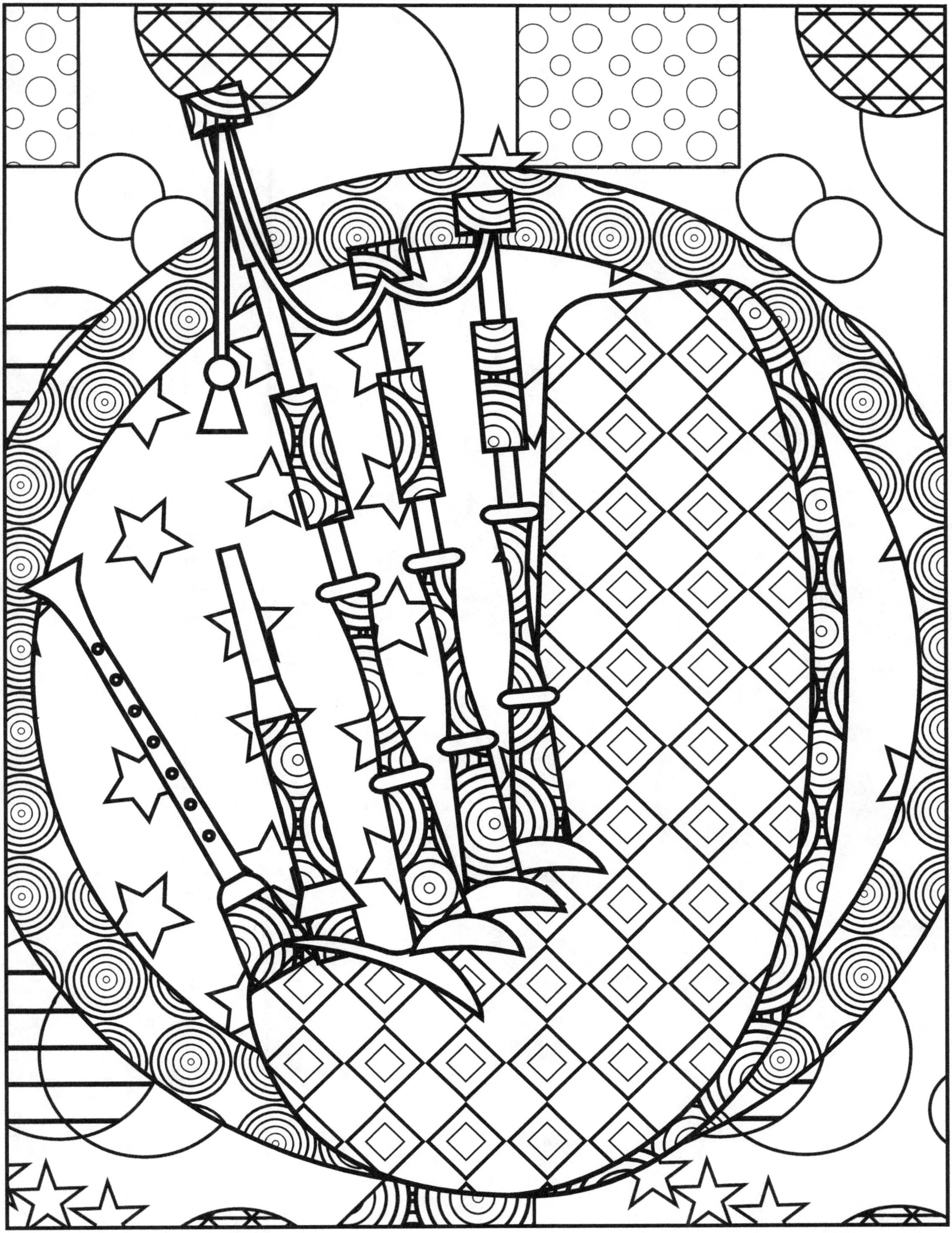

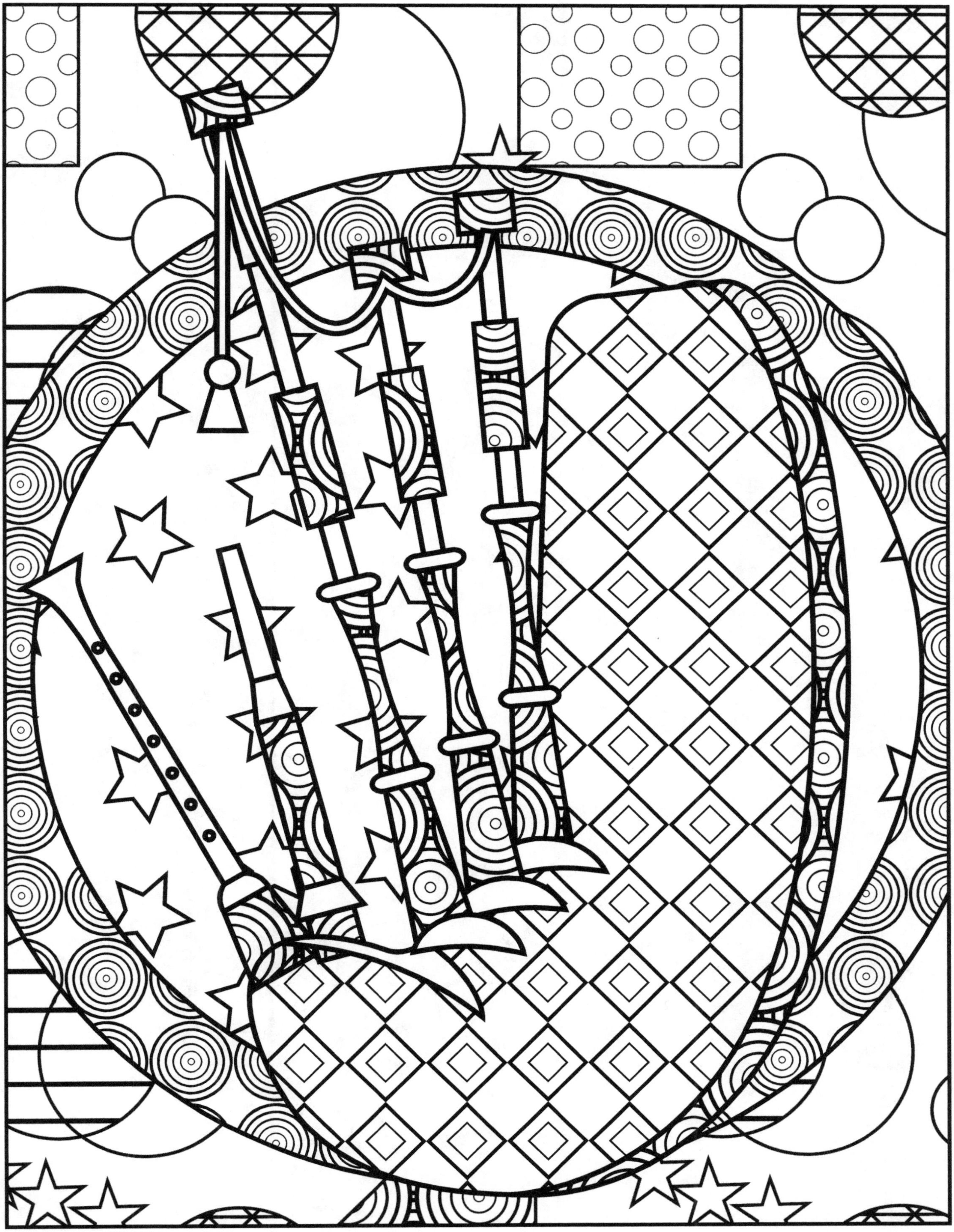

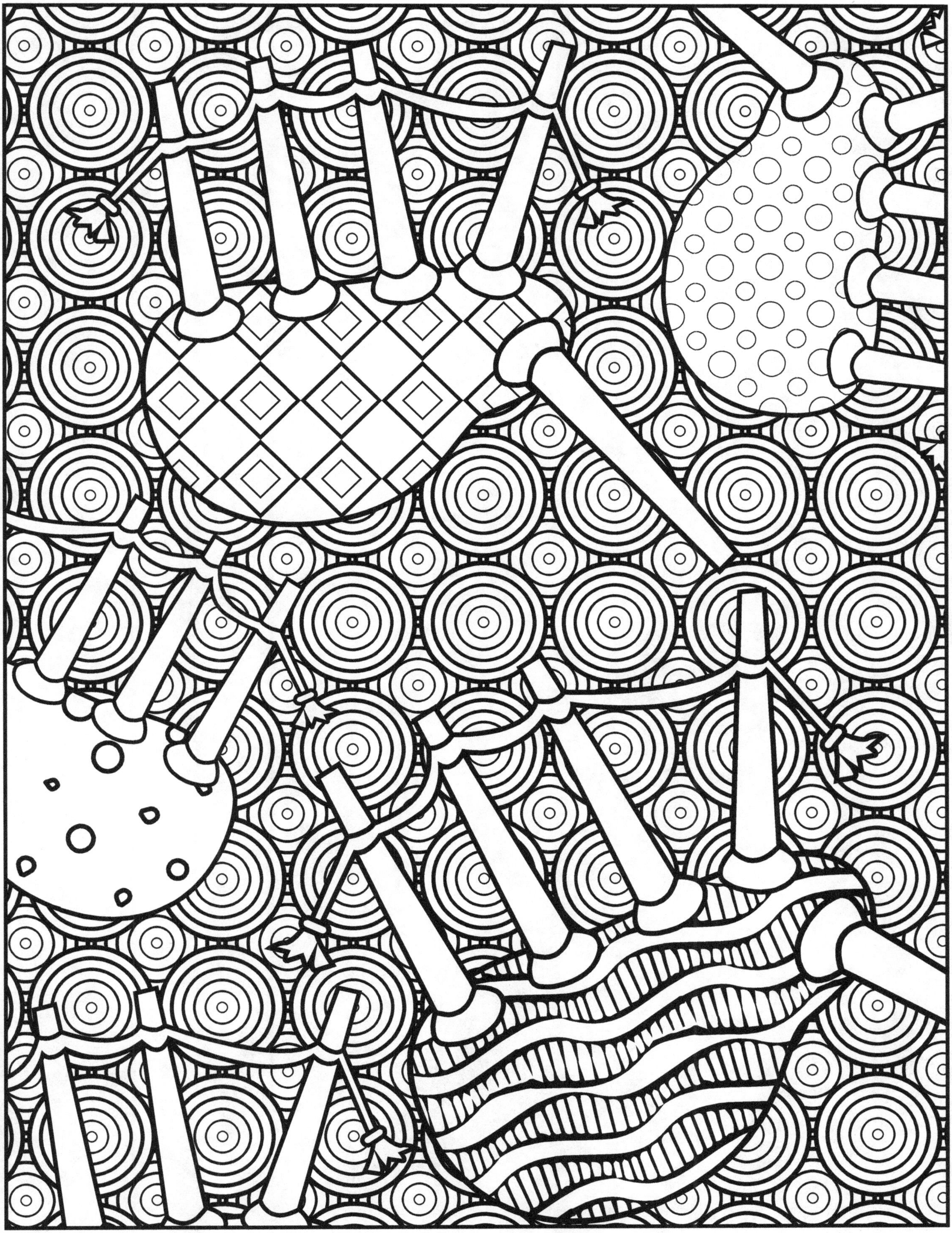

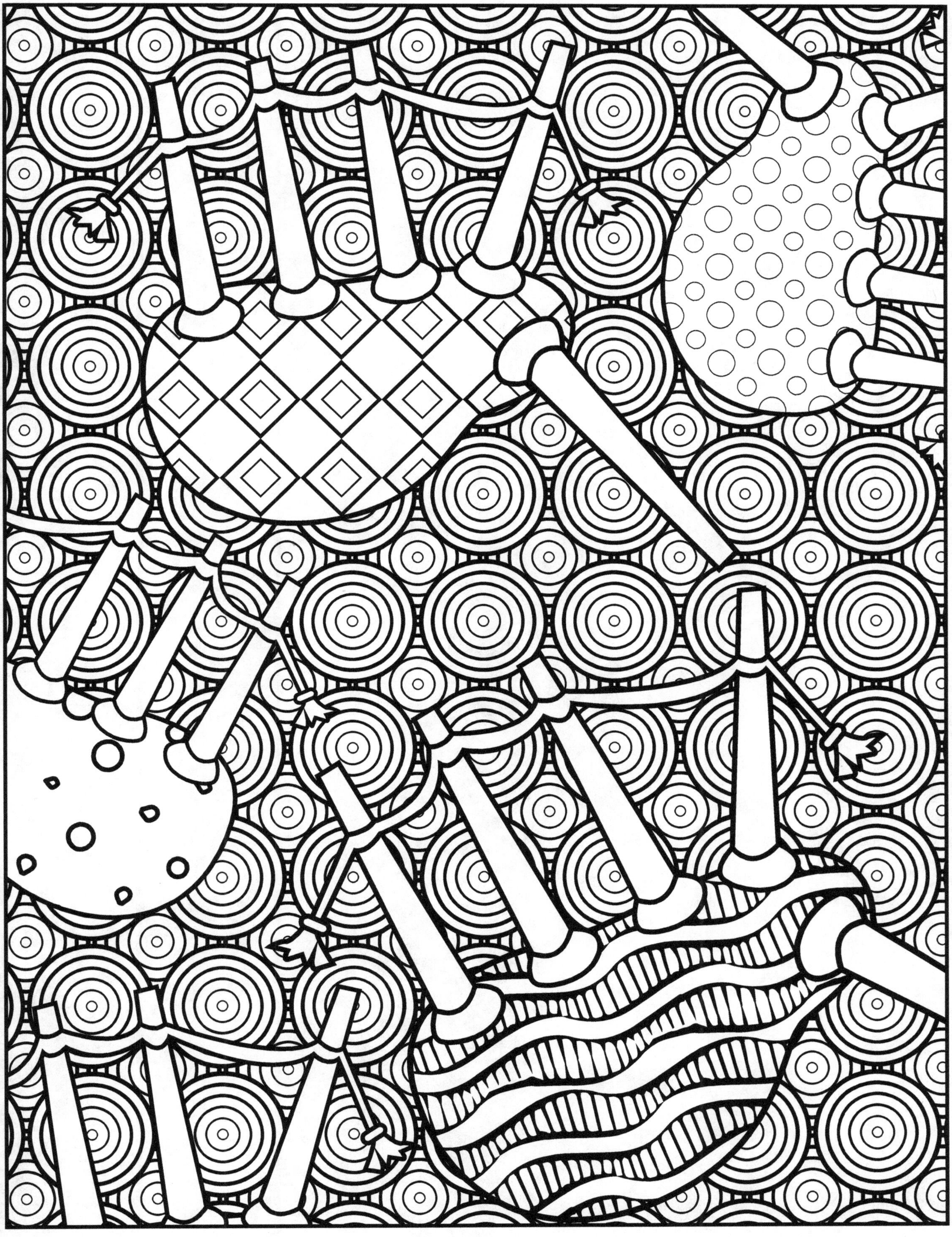

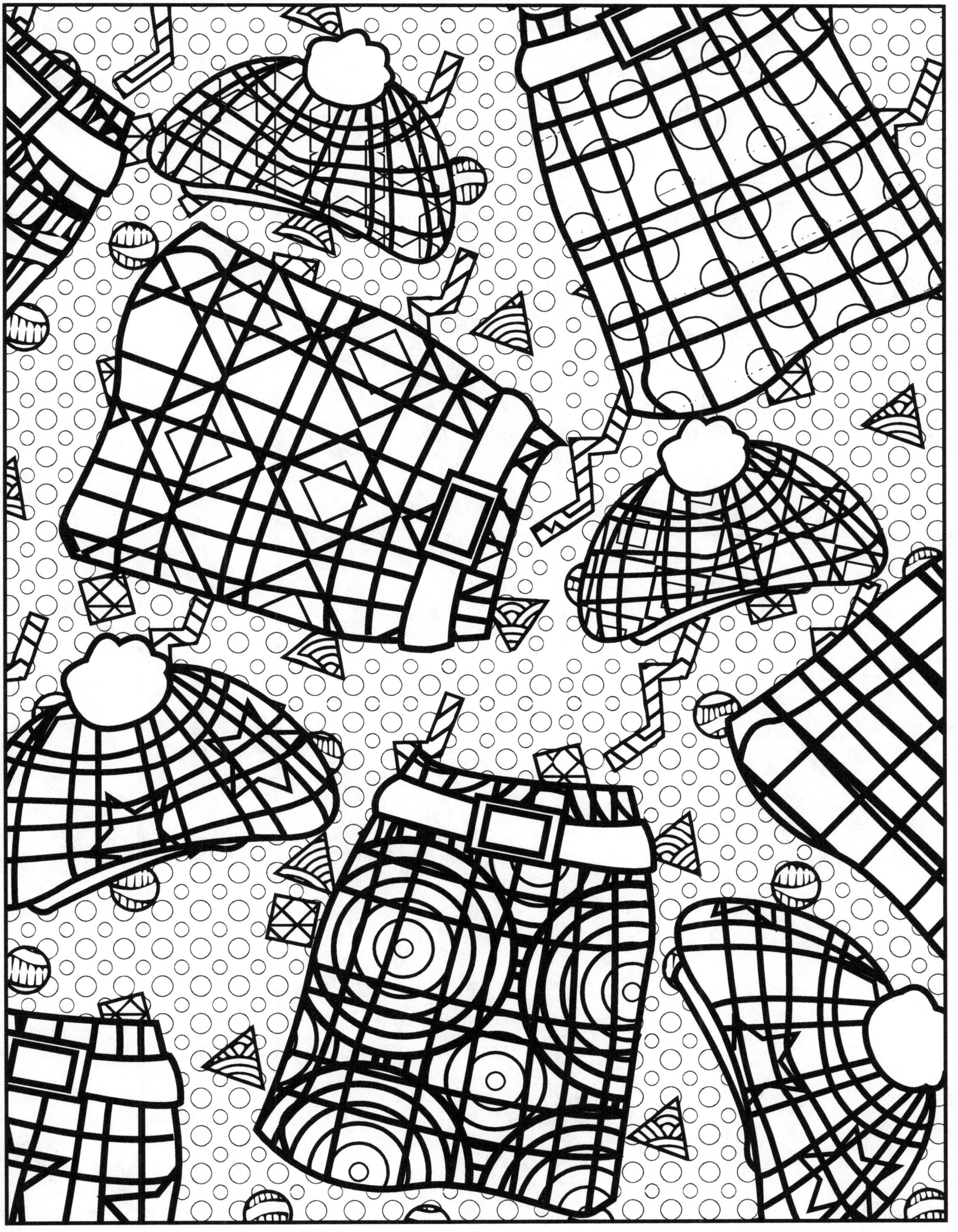

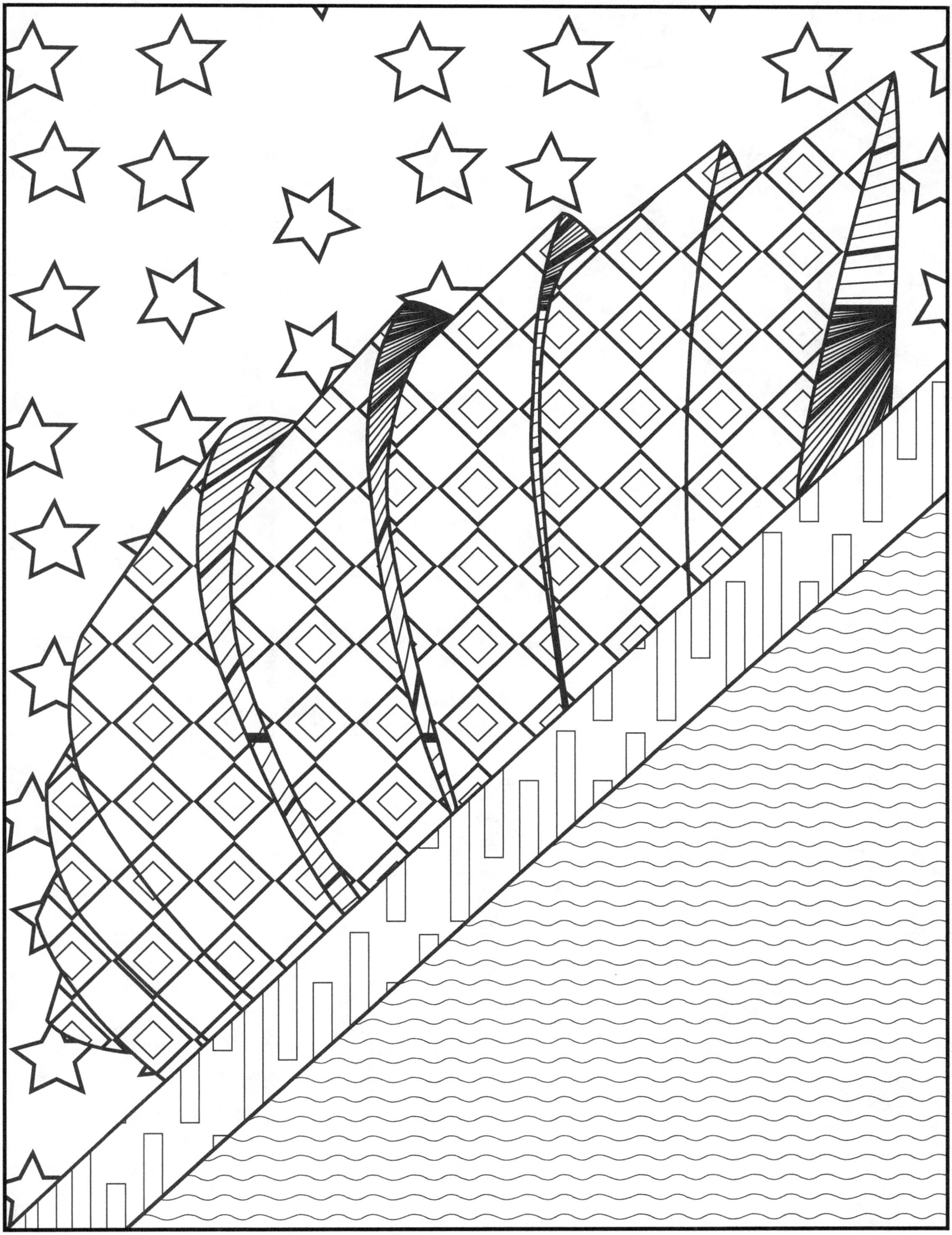

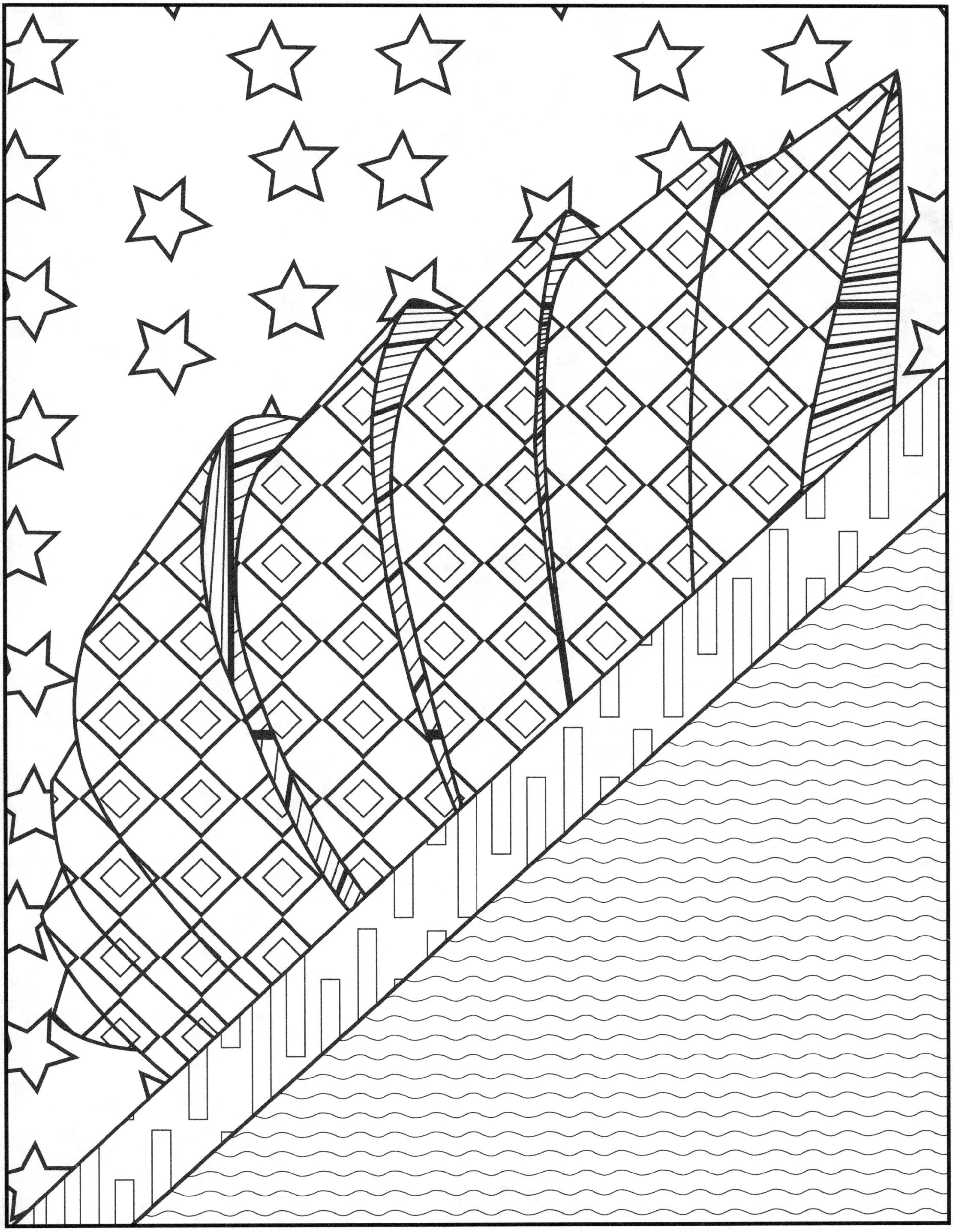

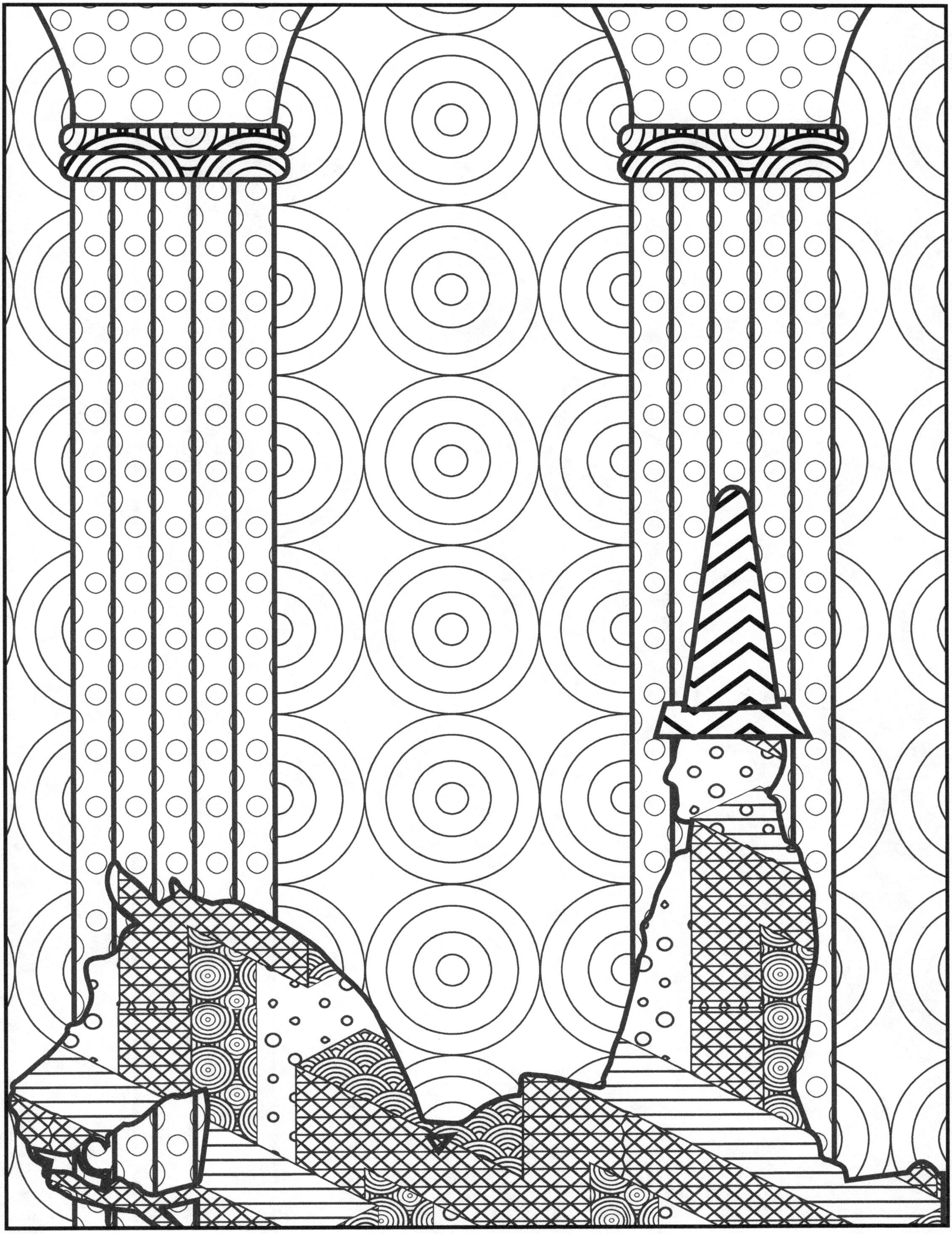

CPSIA information can be obtained
at www.ICGtesting.com
Printed in the USA
BVHW022307200223
658901BV00005B/13

9 781089 879398